CREATION
NOW WITH WORDS

A primer presenting literary evolution based on the great revolution in art during the early 20th Century

Tom Fallon

CREATION NOW WITH WORDS

ISBN: 9781597132183

Library of Congress Control Number: 2020945452

Some word forms in CREATION NOW WITH WORDS have appeared in various print and online literary magazines and in the author's previous book, *NOW - Works on Paper 1976-2006 - Poetry and Antipoetry.*

The author's direction of literary discovery was encouraged by the early maverick literary organization, Maine Writers and Publishers Alliance, specifically Mark Melnicove, Bern Porter, Constance Hunting, Gary Lawless, Lee Sharkey and Sandy Phippen.

Cover Image: *Creation*, Jeff Jacques, Lewiston, Maine

Published by Goose River Press
3400 Friendship Road
Waldoboro Maine 04276-6337

First Edition

Paul Cezanne

...so I am pursuing my researches, and will keep you posted of the results, as soon as my work offers me a trace of satisfaction.

Letter to Ambroise Vollard, 1902

The French painter Paul Cezanne's research and experiments were the foundation for the revolution in art during the 20th Century.

Contents

Foreword

CREATION NOW WITH WORDS is a primer for encouraging independent thought and research relative to literary, word, form, based on the creative revolution in the arts which took place during the early 20th Century.

Nothing is permanent. Heraclitus

There is no must in art because art is free.

Wassily Kandinsky

Those artists who penetrate to the region of that secret place where primeval power nurtures all evolution. Where the power house of all time and space - call it brain or heart of creation - activates every function; who is the artist who would not dwell there?

Paul Klee

What I write, as I have said before, could only be called poetry because there is no other category in which to put it.

Marianne Moore

I encourage a writer to create, experiment and invent, to fail and succeed, with literary, word, form, to embrace the freedom which exists in each person's unique created individuality.

Yes, there are other serious considerations for a writer such as integrity of language, communication, life truth, which I will not relate here. These must not be forgotten -

Tom Fallon

Evolution of TF Word Creation

A writer is free to create new literary forms
or to choose traditional literary forms

Evolution of TF word creation

When presenting the evolution of the word form creation I state that I am beholden to the revolutionary painters of the early 20th Century as well later American writers of the century.

The Norm - The straight left hand margin. My Funny Valentine.

*** TF Experiments begin 1961 ***

Uneven left hand margin, use of the whole page space, positioned in the middle of the whole page space. Wildflowers

Far right hand margin, whole page space, the creation not to be placed on narrow page. Off the road

Lines across the page with uneven margins, nonverbal addition, i.e., performance with energetic voice, hand and body movement.

Shout Black Mingus YEAAAMEN!

Left hand margin, use of whole page space, increased spacing between lines, for slower reading, performing. On this first morning

Middle page position, uneven margins, wide spacing between words, lines, intensity of reading. In the source

Complete use of the whole page space, no margin considerations, word, phrase, sentence spacing improvised. Girl in a small town

USE OF WHOLE PAGE SPACE NO RIGHT OR LEFT HAND MARGIN WORDS PHRASES SPACED IMPROVISED WITH PERFORMANCE
IMPROVISATION FURTHER The Perfect Machine

charteng blow it bomb it sweet form right or left hand
margin words, phrase spaced improvised with
words **outside**
charteng

Open literary form - destroy book page for viewing/reading, i.e., word forms not to be read in hand - page sizes from 8 1/2 x 11 to 36 x 48 to be read from wall display only - on paper, canvas, framed, unframed, etc. - words, phrases and sentences, spaces, placed in the space of whole page -

to watch she is here

Open literary form
with word
with visual
additions 13 x 19
or larger horizontal blood involved

Serial form for wall display from 4 x 6 to 24 x 36 - 2, 3, 4 or more pages in line or otherwise on a wall - framed or not - words, phrases, sentences - single pages of different sizes or shapes type, painted on canvas, sculpted, etc

bending

Word performance creation with individual, group, audience, activity

Let us now honor famous poets **was created for one person but may be adapted for more than one**
& groups may actively create with one or more words -
not necessarily as this performance - using various art materials
i.e., pencil, crayons, ink, paint, magazine newspaper
cut outs, cloth, &c

Single words or phrases in the space of the page she a young woman

Speak words a word an idea think visual non - verbal
speak without a word America 1998

A Beautiful Word **revaluation of a word &c Working with a word - reevaluating a word. View at** ***tomfallon.net***

Enlightenment NOW to liberate in time with creation, words.

& examples specific follow…

The straight left hand margin

The Norm

Usually, a poem is created with a straight left hand margin, positioned in the middle of the page, no matter the width of the page. So it is with *My Funny Valentine*.

My Funny Valentine

From Miles Davis

Miles and miles ahead
with a piercing cry
from the gold horn,.
Black face painted blue,
blue, and bloodied red.

Uneven left hand margin, use of the whole page space, positioned in the middle of the whole page space

First break

Artistic ability as a boy encouraged me to think of life as a visual artist. Higher education was directed to conformity as my exposure to modern art had strongly discouraged so I freed myself to my individuality.

My first poem was frustrating as I tried follow sonnet form. Discouraged, I created by breaking the left and right hand margins, placing the word form in middle of the page using the whole space of the page as one would when creating visual art.

So, *WildFlowers* -

Wildflowers

White bark
of birch trees,
black branches
in the field
orange and yellow
wildflowers.

Far right hand margin, whole page space, the creation not to be placed on narrow page

Moving

A word creation to the right hand margin. which meant all the way to the right hand margin of the page, again thinking whole page space, not placed in the middle of a page or on a narrow page.

Off the road

Off the road

walking
off the road

into tall gras
grass,
wild bushes,
ferns green,
dripping
rainwater globules

scooching down,
I am surrounded
by green leaves,
my head equal
to wild
green bushes

tall grasses and ferns,
rainwater globules
held to green leaves
equal to my self

I lay down
in wild green bushes,
tall grass, ferns green,
rainwater globules
splittering down on
my face
under green leaves

I lay down
wet and laughing
in wild green bushes,
tall grass, ferns green, the green

I am wet
and laughing yes
I am alive!

Lines across the page with uneven margins, nonverbal addition, i.e., performance with energetic voice, hand and body movement -

Jazz

an influence on word form - John Coltrane, Thelonious Monk - Charlie Mingus! Mingus high with feeling in his *Wednesday Night Prayer Meeting* performance - not intellectual, sterile, sweet - hot, hot, and free. His exploration of form embodied with strong & joyous emotion - loosen up - break free - **feel** -

So - *Shout Black Mingus YEAAAMEN!*

Yes, we do understood that we human beings can, and do, communicate without speaking words - body movement, hand or arm movement, touch of another person, facial expression, voice variations, etc.

So - *Shout Black Mingus YEAAAMEN!*

POINT - As Marianne Moore told Donald Hall in the Paris Review interview relative to her *In Distrust of Merits*. "I wouldn't call it a poem. It's truthful; it is testimony - to the fact that war is intolerable, and unjust. Haphazard; as form, what has it? It is just a protest-disjointed, exclamatory."

Shout Black Mingus YEAAAMEN!

Hallelujah, Black Brother, SHOUT Hallelujah Black Sister! Shout BLACK - !

Black is the color of my skin – ain't no whitey gonna change my Black Beauty, Lord - !

I say SHOUT, at Wednesday nite prayer meetin' – shout HALLELUJAH LORD, HALLELUHAH - !

Hallelujah Black Sister, dance, DANCE DOWN THE AISLE – SHOUT Black Beauty, BLACK BEAUTY the color of my SKIN - !

Dance, DANCE DOWN THE STREETS, Black Brother, SHOUT LORD, LORD, ain't no Whitey gonna change my BLACK BEAUTY,

WE'RE WITH YOU LORD! YEAAMEN, HALLELUJAH! Black BLACK BLACK BLACK! is the color of my beauty LORD! SHOUT IT! SHOUT IT! DANCE IT - !

YEAAAMEN Lord! HALLELUJAH! BLACK IS THE COLOR OF MY SKIN, YEAMEN, LORD, SHOUT BLACK BEAUTY - !

SHOUT! SHOUT, AND DANCE, THE COLOR OF MY SKIN, BLACK BEAUTY -

BLACK LADY! BLACK BEAUTY! HALLELUJAH! YEAAAMEN - !

Left hand margin, use of whole page space, increased spacing between lines, for slower reading or performing

Quiet

is the other side of human emotion.

Listenting

\- intuiting

quiet -

On Prince Edward Island, Canada, I began *On this first morning*, as every day the ocean moved slowly up on
the shore, the red sand, moved away from the shore, I walking slowly the beach, and continuously the water
breaking up on the shore, receding from the shore, the red sand.

time slow quiet

O n t h i s f i r s t m o r n i n g

On this first morning
before sunrise.

I wake.

Morning air unmoving
over the dark lake.

Water moving slow,
quiet, breaking
under hemlock.

Stones in clear water.

A bird squeals sweet
in the trees.

Quiet.

Across the lake, dark
hemlock.

Water moving slow, quiet,
over stones.

On this first morning
at the lake, dark mountain
distant, grey sky
distant.

Water breaking.

Sun rise,
sky bluing,
without sound.

Morning air unmoving.

Middle page position, uneven margins, wide
spacing between words, lines, intensity of reading

Intensity

as with *Wildflowers* breaking the left hand margin

the boy

moving with spacing between lines for the quiet
embracing the art of the early 20th century first Cezanne then
Van Gogh Picasso Braque & others changing

innovating

in art van Gogh - spaces between words with
In the source

presenting

the intensity of van Gogh

a beloved artist of the boy *first connecting naked with*
the creative
source unafraid unafraid to
unafraid
to
express the force of the creation **NOW**

Read with fierce intensity
And space van Gogh

in the source

After Vincent van Gogh

in the sun –

from his original creation in the source –

from the darkness of his mind a spark –

from the depths of his body fire –

from his hand, seething color –
life exploding on the canvas –

creating in pain –
reality –
in the sun –

revolution –

Complete use of whole page space, no margin considerations, word, phrase, sentence spacing improvised

Girl, in a small town   irrational   space   form

consider space when reading   time   between   words & phrases

relative   to   the length of   spacing

girl in a small town

now / a nice day Living not home Patti was - Late
daughter after school
ordinary - the unusual - today - at the library, football field
well, she just didn't appear and
two strangers / Main Street / beat-up truck
Mom, Mary, preparing spaghetti
after school . coming home Patti
Patti will be home / however
not home, Patti did
Spaghetti's cold calling girlfriend - No
Mary calling girlfriend - no no Patti Patti left
(not home my daughter) late, Ted, Dad? When - what -
and she left Lainie's house two hours
not home after school daughter was not home after school however
no call truck drifting off Main Street
Patti left Patti will be home, Ted / however
Police call Patti left
not home Patti was - Late - Night / searching and / missing / searching
at the edge of town
at the edge of town night falls as the sun sets
(strange truck) Patti left
police combing Hale woods naturally
Patti left Patti is found and she isn't missing now -
in a ditch near Hale woods - Patti is found and she isn't missing -
meet her strange girl Patti left
/ DEAD / RAPED / BEATEN TO DEATH /
when cold spaghetti sits on the kitchen table
drive outta town
Patti's dead?" Night And Patti's Not Home
After School two strangers driving off Main Street
my daughter is dead my daughter is dead my daughter is dead now
not home my daughter Patti was late and the sun has set - night -
Patti Patti left the car is in the driveway at Olsen's and all
the lights in the house are on And the police officer said: Dead,
in Hale woods
Was she raped? We found your daughter, Mr. Olsen /
strangers meet and we think
all the lights were on at the Olsen's house Patti left
not home Patti was - Late
we think we must go now Patti left
/ DEAD / RAPED / BEATEN TO DEATH / strangers now
in a small town Life
after school today meeting finally
- dead off Main street - cars - trucks - passing
"Patti's dead? (now)
"Honey? "Patti's dead? "Raped?

USE OF WHOLE PAGE SPACE NO RIGHT OR LEFT HAND MARGIN WORDS PHRASES

SPACED IMPROVISED WITH PERFORMANCE IMPROVISATION
FURTHER

clearly heard *Webern'sOpus7forpiano & strings* first — time stopped

after hearing time recreated by
Thelonious Monk
toying

with time which kiLLS us thumbing his

nose at time

capture time ***time*** **improvise with** *The Perfect*
Machine

(improvise when reading repeating
raising
lower voice so
whisper)

time with monk

The Perfect Machine

O such a perfect machine!

What is it?

Take it apart –

one piece at a time _ *Break it down –*

one word at a time yes –

lay the pieces – the words – on the desk –

NOW – *put it together – create*

a new mechanism – change perfection

to mark time – to mark time –

TAKE IT A-PART, BROTHER!

Ha! I've got it!

(...you will not know, if you do not...) A p a r t – *S : T : R : E : T : C : H :*

Now! take it – take, it… take......it......a-part a Part – !

Do it again – and again, do it AGAIN..... (– again go in!

GO DOWN! closer closer – closer –) – creation !

space & time.......... Now. *space & time..........* Now.

charteng   blow it   bomb it sweet form   **right or left hand**
margin   words, phrase   spaced improvised with

words

outside

after reading Marianne Moore's 2 points in PR 61 interview
w Donald Hall about her literary form not
not being poetry in two replies but she had no other name for it & i
took out all stops   ***w Charteng***

Mingus blowing   Monk opening space & time

o pening space & time

possibility   search
investigation -   exploration
uncovering creation   originality
invent

CREATION   with words   which means
destruction
of old form   now   or which means now
which means now

creation! *(as original*

charteng

WITHIN

with all

green

quiet

as

and

implying

refusing

a

fixed

harshness

with in

speeding over the highway

making light

effusive

this

lighter green

and

forced

flowering a blue

with in

Here we are at a crossroads with *Charteng* - destroyed literary form almost completely. Where do we go? We must remember the word, literature, is meant for communication, in various ways. What now?

Experiment - ***Create -*** ***as***

Open literary form - destroy book page for viewing/reading, i.e., word forms not to be read in hand - page sizes from 8 1/2 x 11 to 36 x 48 to be read from wall display only - on paper, canvas, framed, unframed, etc. - words, phrases, sentences, spaces, placed in the space of whole page - on paper, canvas, etc., framed, unframed, etc.

space between words phrases sentences
word blocks time

for wall hanging in a gallery – stop a person
human
being

stop for the whole take time to grasp understand

embrace

say something with time and space say something with space
and time

say something

and beyond

horizontal size 11 x 17 is

to watch she is here

to watch   to be
she is here   sitting up
sitting   in   bed
sun   the window beside the bed
the window beside her   and, sun is coming in the window

her hand moves as she speaks   speaking   she moves
slowly   in   bed
in the sun light
animated, she is
with the sun light   but she does not stand
and speaking, she smiles   she did walk   she does not walk
lying in the bed
room unfamiliar
she is familiar

it is not unexpected   she is speaking, moving her hand, gesturing, smiling

the window is clean and the sun shines through the window into the room
and the sun is shining this afternoon on the trees in to the room
he is sitting in the chair next to the bed   next to her
sun warm on his shoulders through the window
watching her   listening, to her   to her words
the room is warm   (she is hopeful
and it is the first time she has sat up
the sun is yellow warm
a yellow color
the room is open   even unfamiliar

the room is not dark
(another time   rain falling and the room was dark
she smiles   and he laughs then
(there is not much pain now
she has forgotten the past three days
sitting in the sun light
(agony   she smiles and her face colors
she relaxes, smiling

the man sees the light orange color in the woman's face then   he sees   (he hopes
the sun is hot on his back

with the sun light in the room   she is open   she is full,   and it is warm

Open literary form
with word
with visual
additions

13 x 19
or larger

blood involved

horizontal

i was afraid   i was a child   i was afrad of dying   i knew
oblivion

blood involved

when he backed the car down the driveway, he ran over his three year old grandson, crushing his skull: the boy died immediately

I believed in God as a child
I have always believed in God
I believe in God now

blood gushing from his mouth

immor
y

For God so loved the world that He gave His only begotten Son,
that whoever believes in Him should not perish but have everlasting life.

blood gushing from his neck

blood gushing from the hole

blood everywhere in the room

To me the only success, the only greatness, is immortality.
James Dean

QuickTime™ a
TIFF (LZW) decom
are needed to see th

blood on the walls behind him

blood splattered on the wall when he fired the shotgun in

he said he wanted to kill her when the policeman cuffed him

in the street she was bleeding from three stab wounds

he shouted, I wanted to kill the goddamn fucking bitch

the kids were playing in the yard together
when I went out to the garden for
some cucumbers and lettuce and tomatoes

blood everywhere

yes, I am afraid   before life I knew nothing   I see nothing after life   ceath   I do not not want to die

blood

Serial form for wall display from 4 x 6 to 24 x 36 - 2, 3, 4 or more pages in line or otherwise on a wall - framed or not - words, phrases, sentences single pages different sizes or shapes type, painted on canvas, sculpted, etc literary form with word, with visual additions - 13 x 19 or larger

bending

19 framed 8 1/2 x 11 varied placement on wall as necessary

bending

the whole, which

i an uncertain
  can be

internal bending
    seems to be

with slow falling snow
is all morning

am watching now, and gain fall

snowflakes floating

not falling heavy thickly
as during the dark night

twisting, on a slant, or
is it straight

i cannot be certain of any
straight down falling snow flakes

straight

falling on me if
i am outside the house
as i am outside, often

...Cont'd to 19

Word performance creation with individual, group, audience, activity

One person individual

Let us now honor famous poets **was created for one person but may be adapted for more than one as you**

Groups

may actively create with one or more words -
not necessarily as this performance -
using various art materials i.e., pencil, crayons, ink, paint, magazine newspaper cut outs, cloth, &c

by creating

poetry

today may not be necessary as it naturally was *so*

word performance piece "Let us honor famous poets…"

we die, & are buried &c

the past is the past *we all will die*

change is normal ***funerals are normal***
flowers on the grave

and we leave the cemetery alive

"Let us now honor famous poets..."

Materials

Hardbound copy of Palgrave's The Golden Treasury

Trash barrel. Or city street.

Setting

Room interior or city street.

Action

From a random page of the book read without emphasis a poet's name followed by one or more literary lines.

Tear out the page and drop into trash can. Read, tear, twenty or more pages from the book in this manner.

Drop remaining pages in trash can and state naturally,"Poetry is dead."

Or

Walk a city street reading poets' names and lines and drop pages to sidewalk or street,

Drop remaining pages on sidewalk or street and state naturally,"Poetry is dead."

Single words or phrases in the space of the page

One day I began to think of the significance of the word, language, which we human beings depend on in so many ways. I narrowed this direction to my last illness when I would no longer be able to create sentences. *What word would I want to scrawl as a last word.* So this is one direction -

she a young woman

one must read the space as

much as possible viewing the whole at once even as one reads word

enclosing the word creation whole

in the space

11 x 17 or 13 x 19 or

a size the word artist desires on

she

a young woman

was

a promise

in my mind

here

when i saw her

turn

toward me

i was lifted

light

i looked into her eyes

and

i was freed

warmed

one .

she

i touched her forearm

i know you, she said

time

Speak words a word an idea *think* visual

non-verbal speak without a word

(*America 1998*)

A Beautiful Word

is available online at tomfallon.net

Introduction

One Friday, when reading the New York Times, I noticed the single words and short phrases in film advertisements. I wondered if I could create with single words. I began to position single words on 8 1/2 x 11 sheets.

I graduated to include short phrases, then increased the size of the single words and phrases, positioning the larger words on large sized sheets, up to 4 feet wide, these creations to be viewed on the wall.

The first word I explored was the word "God." I followed with the word death. Both words, as you know, can be words of energy and depth for human beings. The word death is also a negative word.

One day, still relating to death I associated it with a particularly strong negative word. There was no doubt of the word's negativity and its energy as it was used in our everyday life. The word was fuck.

I began to create, to explore the word. At one point I discovered the word fuck had a positive value. While that positive value is non-existent or weak for many, it exists in the word as it is associated with sex and love. I moved forward slowly with an eye to a revaluation of the word fuck from within itself.

Move forward slowly - with a study, followed by The Word, a text piece from initial work with the word fuck, then 27 studies followed by another text piece,The Kiss, ending the exploration with 9 studies.

See *A Beautiful Word* at the link tomfallon.net if you wish.

And this is not the end of creation, evolution, for you will create, evolve, recreate, and she will create, evolve, recreate and creation wil continue...

Afterword

What is the point? You are a creator - with words. A creator -

A - Creation - point from Paul Klee, 20th Century Swiss painter.

Those artists who penetrate to the region of that secret place where primeval power nurtures all evolution. Where the power-house of all time and space - call it brain or heart of creation - activates every function; who is the artist who would not dwell there?

The source of a creative human being as well as of creation.

B - Direction of a a creative word person

To maintain integrity and freedom as an individual creator who draws from the creation source. To defend your integrity from those who wish to neuter, water down, corrupt, it. Individuals and organizations exist with that goal whether from ignorance, personal financial gain or control of others. This situation has existed even in primitive societies.

If you maintain integrity, freedom as an individual creator, you will maintain the integrity of language you draw from creation.

C - What compromises will you make with your word creating to be accepted, to become successful financially, to gain fame?

A writer must always be free to create a new literary form or to choose traditional literary forms. A writer, as individual, must always be free to create.

So be it.

Tom Fallon

References &c

Walt Whitman - Urge and urge and urge, Always the procreant urge of the world.

Claude Debussy - I am increasingly convinced that music is not, in essence, a thing which can be cast into a traditional and fixed form.

Victor Cousins - L'art pour l'art.

Hans Jean Arp - I wanted to find another order, another value for man in nature. I wanted to create new appearances, to extract new forms from man.

Wassily Kandinsky - There is no must in art because art is free.

Paul Klee - Those artists who penetrate to the region of that secret place where primeval power nurtures all evolution. Where the power-house of all time and space - call it brain or heart of creation - activates every function; who is the artist who would not dwell there?

Ezra Pound - Make it new.

William Carlos Williams - All the ways and means we have of writing just go to prove that no one has yet discovered any one best way. Every creative writer will experiment, try out new techniques.

John Cage - If this word "music" is sacred and reserved for eighteenth- and nineteenth-century instruments, we can substitute a more meaningful term: organization of sound.

Richard Kostelanetz - Perhaps the most accurate term for my imaginative endeavors would be 'Language Art.'

Matthew Zapruder - John Ashbery is one of the most lauded poets yet his work defies traditional expectations for what poems should do. At times likened to montage, at others to abstraction in painting, his poems take many different forms but could be said to be more like assemblages of language…

MARIANNE MOORE INTERVIEW

Let me present other points made by Moore in the interview with Donald Hall for the Paris Review, Winter, 1961

Hall: One time I heard you give a reading , and I think you said you didn't like "In Distrust of Merits," which is one of your most popular poems.

Moore: I do like it; it is sincere but I wouldn't call it a poem. It's truthful; it is testimony - the fact that war is intolerable, and unjust.

Hall: How can you call it not a poem, on what basis?

Moore: Haphazard; as form, what has it? It is just a protest - disjointed, exclamatory. Emotion overpowered me. First this thought and then that.

Hall: What was your reaction when H.D. and Bryher brought out your first collection, which they called *Poems*, in 1921...

Moore: To issue my slight product - conspicuously tentative - seemed to me premature. I disliked the term "poetry" for any but Chaucer's or Shakespeare' or Dante's. I do not now feel quite my original hostility to the word, since it is a convenient almost unavoidable term for the thing (although hardly for me) my observations, experiments in rhythm, or exercise in composition, What I write, as I have said before, could only be called poetry because there is no other category in which to put it.

References &c 2

I think the arts since the revolution in the early 20th Century support the freedom and integrity of a person's creative individuality. Consider the following resources and others...

Text Sound Texts by Richard Kostelanetz as well as *Visual Literature Criticism, The Old Poetries and The New, The Avant-Garde Tradition in Literature*
Revolution of the Word 1914-1945 edited by Jerome Rothenberg
Speaking Pictures edited by William Klondez
Sounds That Arouse Me by Bern Porter
ABC of Reading by Ezra Pound and other essays
T. S. Eliot, William Carlos Williams, Marianne Moore, Hart Crane and other writers of that generation
Dada and Surrealism edited by Dawn Ades
Pop Art edited by Christopher Finch
20th Century American Art edited Erika Doss
Dada Art and Anti-art edited by Hans Richter
Marinetti - Selected Writings edited by R. W. Flint
Complete Writings on Art of Kandinsky

A creative writer should have the freedom to invent any literary form necessary for a particular creative work following the example of the freedom in creation which presents a multiplicity of different life forms. A creative writer should not be bound to employ only forms of past literature by any person or organization.

I am an artist of paint, making discoveries.

Helen Frankenthaler

Every so often a painter has to destroy painting. Cezanne did it. Picasso did it with cubism, then Pollock did it. He busted our idea of a picture all to hell.

Willem de Kooning

bio

inquisitive troublesome 6 yr old in 1942 1st grade teacher separatd tf
fr other students to color
a yellow rabbit &
developd visual art direction secondary school years

browsd public library bord w hs @ 16 discovrd Thomas Craven's *Men of Art* great artists of past stimulated by modern
art revolutionaries esp van Gogh &c !

left 2 colleges disturbd re success conformity & art pkg enlisting US Air Force stationd Long Island discovrd foreign films
NYC art & theater Ezra Pound's *ABC of Reading*
jumpd writing

found Maine woman providing stability connectd w MWPA radical inmigrants support 4 free literary direction discover
jazz jazz modern classical music Off Off Broadway
theater 60s&70s
continud writing exploring literary form
rejecting settlement Boston NYC speed Seventies chaos

discoverd generation of American writers before
William Carlos Williams Marianne Moore Hart Crane
T. S. Eliot Dick Higgins Bern Porter &c
supporting exploration of literary form
Red Dust NYC publishd "Pregnant Man 1"

one day Marianne Moore's interview w Donald Hall - "I was not
writing poetry…" revelation

as creatd natural direction for visual art basic principle of word creation reinforcd by
20th Century art revolt ban creation

or bio

Tom Fallon subtitled his first book "Selected Poems, Half-poems and Non-poems" in 1978 as he established his direction to explore poetry and literary form rather than to employ only traditional poetry forms. At the time he was associated with and supported by the early Maine Writers and Publishers Alliance. Fallon's subsequent books, *Pregnant Man 1* in Red Dust 3, *The Man on the Moon* and *NOW* continued his exploration to the point where he posited a new literary category, chartteng, after discovering Marianne Moore's statement in an interview with Donald Hall for the Paris Review: "What I write, as I have said before, is only called poetry because there is no other category in which to put it.." The term relates to the already established categories in the fine arts such as collage, environments, etc. Fallon's creation has also been affected by his exposure to modern painting, modern jazz, experimental classical music, happenings and Off Off Broadway theater of New York in the Seventies. His explorations have led him to use the "whole page space" from 8 1/2 to 24" x 36" size pages, titled wall writings, to be displayed and read only on the wall. His primary focus is, of course, on the freedom of the individual artist, the writer of words, to explore or experiment when necessary without restriction of form as the visual artist has had that direction since the early 20th Century. Literary influences have included William Carlos Williams, Marianne Moore, Bern Porter, Dick Higgins, Ezra Pound, Charles Olson, Richard Kostelanetz, Bern Porter and others.

I am creation. You are creation.

Tom Fallon

www.ingramcontent.com/pod-product-compliance
Lightning Source LLC
Chambersburg PA
CBHW071519030726
47593CB00003B/1333

* 9 7 8 1 5 9 7 1 3 2 1 8 3 *